HAVING FUN WITH FELTING

By Dana Meachen Rau • Illustrated by Kathleen Petelinsek

CHERRY LAKE PUBLISHING • ANN ARBOR, MICHIGAN

CHERRY LAKE
Publishing

Published in the United States of America by Cherry Lake Publishing
Ann Arbor, Michigan
www.cherrylakepublishing.com

Photo Credits: Page 4, ©Artex67/Shutterstock; page 5, ©Babich Alexander/Shutterstock; page 6, ©berna namoglu/Shutterstock; page 7, ©djem/Shutterstock; page 29, ©misastudio/Shutterstock

Library of Congress Cataloging-in-Publication Data
Rau, Dana Meachen, 1971–
  Having fun with felting / by Dana Meachen Rau.
    pages cm. — (How-to library)
  Includes bibliographical references and index.
  Audience: 4 to 6.
  ISBN 978-1-63362-370-5 (lib. bdg.) — ISBN 978-1-63362-426-9 (pdf) — ISBN 978-1-63362-398-9 (pbk.) — ISBN 978-1-63362-454-2 (ebook)
  1. Felt work—Juvenile literature. 2. Felting—Juvenile literature. I. Title.
  TT849.5.R38 2016
  746'.0463—dc23   2015003483

Cherry Lake Publishing would like to acknowledge the work of the Partnership for 21st Century Skills. Please visit www.p21.org for more information.

Printed in the United States of America
Corporate Graphics
July 2015

TABLE OF CONTENTS

Fiber Felting Fun…4
From Sheep to Fabric…6
Basic Supplies…8
Flat Felted Fabric…10
Imaginative Image…14
Felted BBs and Balls…15
Felted Fruit…17
Bull's-Eye Beads…20
Bull's-Eye Bracelet…23
Felted Flowers…24
Felted Snowman…27
Wooly Wonders…29

Glossary…30
For More Information…31
Index…32
About the Author…32

Fiber Felting Fun

You can felt all sorts of interesting designs.

When people think of art, tools such as pencils and paper, paintbrushes and paint, or stone and chisels may come to mind. But some of the most beautiful pieces of art are made from much softer things. **Fiber** art is the practice of creating things from fabric, thread, yarn, and other soft materials. This includes everything from quilts and tapestries to needlepoint, rugs, and clothing.

People have been using natural fibers to make things for centuries. Silk, cotton, flax, and wool fibers can be sewn, woven, or knit together to make fabric. One particular type of fabric—felt—has been used for about 2,500 years.

Long ago, people often moved from place to place instead of settling in permanent homes. These **nomads** needed portable shelter, so they made felt from wool and used it to build tents. The felt tents were easy to take down, pack up, and move to a new location. The use of felt spread as different nomadic cultures traded their goods and ideas. Felt was eventually used to make everything from blankets and coats to carpets and even armor.

Today, felt still has lots of uses. Have you ever looked inside a piano? You'll find felt pads under the keys. Hats, athletic pads, and pool tables are made using felt. Felt pads protect floors from furniture. You can erase a chalkboard with a felt eraser.

Not only can you make things out of felt yourself, but you can make the fabric itself, too. Have fun felting fibers together to form unique and useful creations!

Felt is a very common material for making hats.

From Sheep to Fabric

After a sheep's wool is sheared, it begins growing
back. The process can start all over again!

Wool fibers come from sheep. Wool is neither hair nor fur,
though it is similar to both. People cut wool from sheep using
scissorlike blades called shears. After the wool has been removed
from the sheep, it is washed. Then it goes through a process
called **carding**. This untangles and separates the wool fibers.
The fibers are then made into **roving**. A roving is a long rope
of wool fibers that have been gathered together. Roving is often
spun into yarn, which can be knit or woven to make fabrics.

Felt is made differently than other wool fabrics. It is not knitted or woven. Instead, it is made of loose wool fibers that lock together after being exposed to heat, water, and pressure. There are two types of felting. They are called dry felting and wet felting. In this book, we will focus on wet felting. If you could look at wool with a microscope, you would see little scales on each fiber. When the wool gets wet and warm, these scales lift up. They attach to the scales on other fibers, locking the strands together. Because of this process, felt cannot unravel like other types of fabric.

Wool fibers come in a huge variety of colors.

Basic Supplies

To make felt, you need four basic things: wool, water, soap, and **friction**.

Wool

Visit a local yarn store to buy roving. You might also find it for sale at large craft stores. Roving comes in many colors and styles. Look for Merino wool. It felts well and is easiest to find.

Water and Soap

You will use both warm and cold water for the projects in this book. It will help if you can set up your workspace near a sink. Cover this space with a plastic tablecloth for easy cleanup. Keep towels handy to **absorb** excess water. Liquid dish detergent or shampoo makes the best soap. You will also need a plastic spray bottle for wetting the felt and a plastic bin for dunking.

Friction

Bumpy surfaces such as bubble wrap (with large or small bubbles) or nonslip shelf liner will make it easier to create friction for your projects.

Other Stuff

To keep fibers from moving around as you work, you will need a piece of netting or tulle (the type of fabric used to make ballet tutus). You will also need two small pieces of plastic. The easiest way to get this plastic is to cut the seams off of a zip-top bag.

When you make a flat project, you will roll each piece of felt into a bundle. You will need a **cylindrical** shape to form these bundles. A piece of a pool noodle works best. You can also use a wooden dowel as long as it is at least 1 inch (2.5 centimeters) thick. Use rubber bands to hold the bundles together.

A cooling rack (the type used to cool cookies) makes a good drying spot for your projects. The rack will allow air to reach the felt from above and below. It is best to let most pieces dry overnight if possible.

Other craft and office supplies necessary for these projects include pipe cleaners, a craft knife and safe cutting surface, masking tape, craft felt, yarn, pencils, paper, scissors, tacky glue, a hot glue gun, and a ruler.

Necessary sewing supplies include a needle, thread, and fabric scissors.

Flat Felted Fabric

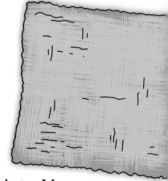

This is the basic process to create a piece of felted fabric. You can use this fabric for other projects described in this book. If you prefer, you can also use it to form your own interesting creations!

Materials

- Plastic tablecloth
- Pencil, paper, ruler
- Gallon-size zip-top bag cut along the seams to make two pieces of plastic
- Wool roving in any color or mix of colors you wish
- Piece of tulle or netting measuring 10 inches (25 cm) square
- Plastic spray bottle filled with warm, soapy water
- Hand towels
- Sheet of bubble wrap measuring 12 inches (30.5 cm) by 24 inches (61 cm)
- Piece of pool noodle measuring 12 inches (30.5 cm) long
- 4 to 6 rubber bands
- Cooling rack

Steps

1. Prepare your workspace by laying out the tablecloth. Draw a shape that is about 8 inches (20 cm) square on the paper. This will be your **template**. Place it on top of

the tablecloth. Then place one of the pieces of plastic on top of the paper.

2. Gently pull a thin tuft of fibers from the end of the roving. Do this by using the thumb and index finger of one hand to hold on near the end of the roving and pulling the fibers straight out to the side with the thumb and index finger of your other hand.

3. Starting in the upper left corner of the square, lay down a tuft of fibers **horizontally**. Continue laying tufts down the left edge until you reach the bottom. Start a second column next to the first, overlapping the ends of the fibers slightly. Then add a third column (and a fourth if needed) to fill up the square shape. Add bits of roving to any bare spots.

4. For the next layer, you will lay the fibers in the opposite direction. Starting in the upper left corner, lay down a tuft of fibers **vertically**. Continue laying tufts across the top edge until you reach the right side. Then start a second row below the first, overlapping the ends of the fibers slightly. Add a third row (and a fourth if needed) to complete the second layer. Fill in any bare spots.

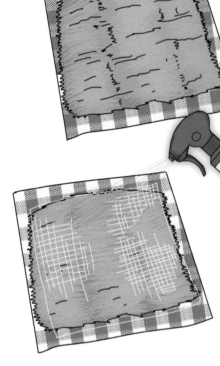

5. Repeat step 3 to add a third horizontal layer to the piece. You will have three layers in all. Remove the template from underneath the plastic.

6. Place the netting on top of the fibers to help hold them in place. Wet the fibers by spraying them with the warm, soapy water. Press the netting down to get out all of the air. Make sure the piece is completely wet but not overly soaked. Use the towel to absorb any extra water.

7. Use your fingertips to rub the fibers through the netting for a few minutes. This will create friction on the fibers. Apply light pressure at first so the fibers don't move around too much. Peel up the netting every so often to be sure the fibers aren't sticking to it.

8. When the fibers start clinging together, remove the netting and fold in the piece's rough edges. Replace the netting and keep rubbing.

9. After a few more minutes, you'll need to flip the piece over to the other side. Remove the netting and place the second piece of plastic over the piece. Flip it over and remove the first piece of plastic. Place the netting on top, then rub this side for a few more minutes. Try pulling lightly on the surface. If the fibers come up easily, rub some more. If they mostly stay in place, you are ready to move on to **fulling**.

10. Fulling is when you provide even more friction to get the fibers to shrink and lock together. Lay the bubble wrap on a surface with the bubble side facing up. Remove the netting and gently lift the piece from the plastic and transfer it to the center of the bubble wrap. Starting at the bottom, roll the bubble wrap and felt piece around the pool noodle until you reach the top. Use rubber bands to secure the roll into a tight bundle.

11. Roll the bundle back and forth about 60 times or for about one minute. As you roll, use long strokes and apply pressure. You can do this on a table with your hands and arms or on the floor with your feet!

Rotate piece 90 degrees

12. Unroll the bundle. Lift the piece, smooth out any wrinkles, flip it over, and reposition it on the bubble wrap by turning it 90 degrees. Soak up any extra water with the towel. Roll the bundle back up, secure it with rubber bands, and roll it about 60 times again. Continue unrolling, repositioning, and rerolling the bundle 6 to 10 times. You are done when the fibers don't come apart when you pinch the felt. If they do, keep on rolling!

13. When you are happy with the piece, rinse it under cold water in the sink to remove the soap. Roll it into a towel to squeeze out extra water. Finally, lay the finished piece on a cooling rack and allow it to dry completely.

Imaginative Image

Add bits of yarn and roving to flat felted fabric to create a beautiful piece of art. Wool yarn will cling best, but novelty yarns can add extra flair, too! Let the colors of the wool and yarn inspire you.

Materials

- Materials for Flat Felted Fabric (see page 10)
- Small strands of wool and novelty yarn

Steps

1. Lay out three layers of roving as described in steps 1 through 5 of the Flat Felted Fabric project. Add tufts of other colors of roving and scraps of yarn on top of the third layer.
2. Sprinkle some strands of roving over the image—not so much that you cover it, but enough to help hold the various decorations onto the surface.
3. Wet, press, rub, roll, flip, rinse, and dry the piece as described in steps 6 through 13 in the Flat Felted Fabric project.

DISPLAY IDEAS
To display your fabric art, you can frame it, hang it from a dowel r[...] as a wall hanging, or se[...] it onto a throw pillow.

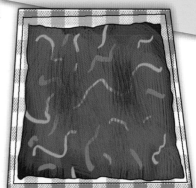

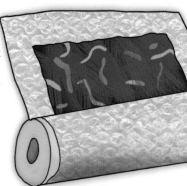

Felted BBs and Balls

You can magically transform a handful of loose wool fibers into tight, hard balls of all sizes, from tiny BBs to tennis balls. Think of all the things you can make with these little spheres of wool!

Materials

- Hand towels
- Nonslip shelf liner or bubble wrap
- Plastic bin filled with warm, soapy water
- Wool roving in any color or mix of colors you wish
- Cooling rack

Steps

1. Prepare your workspace by laying out a towel. Place the shelf liner or bubble wrap on top. Set the plastic bin next to it.
2. Pinch a bunch of tufts from the roving. Lay some in your palm facing one way, then lay some facing the other way. Continue laying them down in opposite directions until you have filled up your hand.

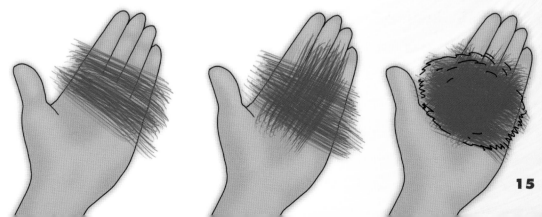

3. Roll the fibers between your palms until they form a loose ball. Dip the ball into the warm water and continue rolling it in your palms. Hold it over the tub to avoid getting water everywhere. As you roll, the fibers will start to mesh together.

4. Continue to roll the ball around in your palms. You can also roll it on the shelf liner to provide more friction. Dunk the ball in the warm water from time to time, and continue rolling until the fibers shrink up and the ball becomes hard.

5. If the ball has any folds, or if you want it to be larger, wrap it with more tufts of roving and continue dunking and rolling until the ball is hard again.

6. When the ball is done, rinse it with cold water. Squeeze it in a towel to absorb the excess water. Finally, place it on a cooling rack to dry completely. This could take as long as 24 hours, depending on the size of the ball.

The amount of roving you use will determine the size of the ball. Three tufts will make a tiny BB-sized ball. Ten tufts will make a much larger one. As mentioned above, you can always add more roving as you go. It's best to start small and add roving until your ball reaches the desired size.

Felted Fruit

Think of all the fruits that are round. There are blueberries, apples, cherries, and many more. You can make a bunch of felted balls, add some stem and leaf details, and display them in a bowl as a felted fruit salad!

Materials

- Materials for Felted BBs and Balls (see page 15); use various colors of roving, such as green for apples, red for cherries, blue for blueberries, purple for plums, orange for oranges, etc.
- Scissors
- Green craft felt
- Toothpicks
- Needle and blue thread
- Tacky glue

Steps

For an apple

1. Follow the steps for the Felted BBs and Balls project on page 15, starting with about 10 tufts of green, yellow, or red roving. Add more as you roll to create an apple-sized ball.
2. Cut a leaf shape out of the craft felt, making sure that one end is extra pointy.

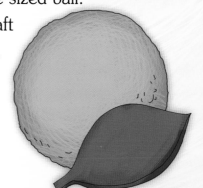

3. Push a toothpick into the top of the apple to make a hole. Remove the toothpick, and then use it to push in the pointy end of the leaf until both the leaf and toothpick are secure. Snip off part of the toothpick with the scissors to make a stem.

For blueberries

1. Follow the steps for the Felted BBs and Balls project on page 15, starting with about three tufts of blue roving. Don't add any extra roving as you work. You want the blueberries to be as small as possible. Repeat the steps for as many blueberries as you wish.
2. Thread the needle and knot the end. Push it up through one of the blueberries from bottom to top. Pull the thread all the way through the berry.
3. Sew crisscrossing lines across the top of the berry to make a star shape. Push the needle back through the center and down to the bottom. Knot the end and snip off any extra thread.

SEWING TIP:
Knot the end of the thread to the ball by making a stitch, threading the needle through the loop, and pulling tight. Repeat.

For 2 cherries

1. Follow the steps for the Felted BBs and Balls project on page 15, starting with about six tufts of red roving. Add more as you roll if needed.
2. Cut two leaf shapes out of the craft felt.
3. Push a toothpick into the top of the cherry. Squeeze a dot of glue on the end of each leaf. Sandwich the top of the toothpick between the gluey ends of the leaves and squeeze them together. Let the glue dry.
4. Repeat to make more cherries.

Bull's-Eye Beads

Have you ever rolled a snake out of clay? You will use the same rolling method for this project. By rolling different colors of roving inside each other, you can make a snake of felted fabric and cut it into beads. Each one will look like a tiny bull's-eye!

Materials

- Plastic tablecloth
- Sheet of bubble wrap or nonslip shelf liner measuring about 12 inches (30.5 cm) square
- Masking tape
- Plastic tub filled with hot, soapy water
- Hand towel
- Three colors of wool roving (referred to as Color One, Color Two, and Color Three)
- Cooling rack
- Ruler
- Craft knife and safe cutting surface

Steps

1. Prepare your workspace by laying out the plastic tablecloth. Tape down the bubble wrap or shelf liner so it doesn't shift around as you work. Set the tub with water to the side. Fill a sink with cold water.
2. Gently pull a piece of roving about 1 inch (2.5 cm) wide and 12 inches (30.5 cm) long from Color One. Lay it on

your work surface horizontally. Use your fingertips to gently roll the length of roving back and forth. This will **compress** the fibers and get out the air. Continue rolling for about 3 minutes. As the fibers start to mesh together, you can apply more pressure. Set the Color One piece aside.

3. Pull small tufts of Color Two from the roving and lay them on the work surface in a long rectangle that is about the same length of the Color One piece, but with the fibers running vertically. Make sure there are no empty spaces.

4. Dip the Color One piece into the tub of hot water. Lay it in the center of the Color Two roving. Gently roll the piece up in the fibers so that it is fully covered. Roll this combined piece on the bubble wrap for about 5 minutes, applying more pressure as the fibers harden. Set it aside.

5. Pull small tufts of Color Three from the roving and lay them on the work surface both horizontally and vertically to make a long rectangle shape.

6. Dip the rolled-up combined piece in the hot water and lay it on top

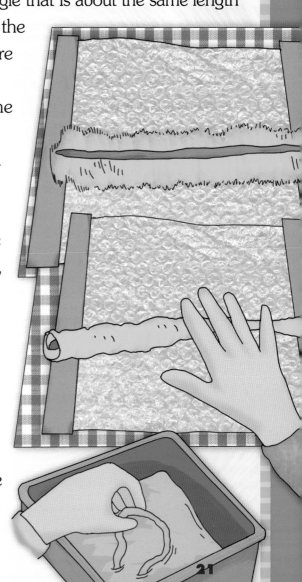

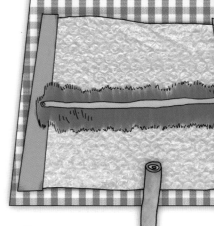

of the Color Three roving. Roll it up into the roving. Roll it up like before, gently at first and applying more pressure as it hardens, for about 5 minutes.

7. Test the hardness of the piece. If it bends when you hold it upright, it isn't ready yet. Dunk the piece into the hot water, then dunk it into the cold water. Pull on the ends of the piece to help squeeze out some of the extra water and stretch the fibers.

If your piece does not stand up like this, repeat step 8 until it does.

8. Back at the work surface, roll the piece back and forth for a few minutes. Then dunk it in hot and cold water again. Repeat as many times as you need to. Test the piece by holding it upright by one end again. If it stands straight up and feels hard, you are done.

9. Roll the piece in a towel and gently squeeze to absorb the extra water. Place it on a cooling rack until it dries completely. This should take about 24 hours.

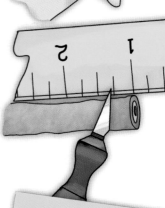

10. Place the piece on a safe cutting surface and gently saw through it near the center using the craft knife. You will see the bull's-eye shape inside! Cut the rest of the piece every 0.25 inches (0.6 cm) to make beads.

Ask an adult to help you use the craft knife. It is very sharp!

Bull's-Eye Bracelet

Sew your Bull's-Eye Beads together and hit the fashion target with this jazzy bracelet.

Materials

- Tape measure
- Needle
- Elastic thread
- 12 to 16 Bull's-Eye Beads (see pages 20–22)
- 12 to 16 plastic seed beads
- Scissors

Steps

1. Measure around your wrist with the tape measure to determine the size of your bracelet.
2. Thread the needle and knot the end. Leave a tail of thread about 1 inch (2.5 cm) long. Poke the needle through the middle of a Bull's-Eye Bead from side to side. Next, string on a seed bead. Continue **alternating** the two types of beads until you reach the length you measured in step 1.
3. Tie the ends of the thread together with a knot. Trim off any excess thread.

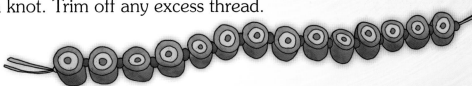

Felted Flowers

Combine Felted Fabric, Felted Balls, and Bull's-Eye Beads to make these lovely flowers to decorate your room.

Materials
- Piece of Flat Felted Fabric (see page 10)
- Scissors
- Two stems (see directions below)
- Hot glue gun
- Two medium-sized Felted Balls (see page 15)
- 12 Bull's-Eye Beads (see page 20)
- Vase (for display)

Steps
1. Cut a circle from the fabric. Cut into the edges to make petal shapes. Use the scissors to snip a small X-shaped hole in the center of the piece. Thread one stem through the X-shaped hole.
2. Squeeze hot glue around the top of the stem and press the sides of the X-shaped hole onto the glue to hold the flower's petals in place.

3. Squeeze a blob of glue into the center of the flower. Stick one of the Felted Balls onto the glue. Then squeeze six dots of glue around the ball and use them to attach six of the Bull's-Eye Beads.

4. Repeat steps 1 through 3 to make another flower. Display them in a vase.

Materials to Make the Stems

- Plastic tablecloth
- Sheet of bubble wrap or nonslip shelf liner measuring about 12 inches (30.5 cm) square
- Masking tape
- Green wool roving
- Pipe cleaner
- Plastic spray bottle filled with warm, soapy water
- Hand towel
- Cooling rack

Steps

1. Prepare your work surface by laying out the tablecloth and taping down the bubble wrap

Ask an adult to help you with the hot glue gun. It can get very hot!

or shelf liner. Pull out tufts of roving and lay them on the work surface both horizontally and vertically to form a long rectangle shape. Place a pipe cleaner in the middle of the rectangle. Gently roll the pipe cleaner up in the fibers, making sure that it is completely covered.

2. Wet the fibers by spraying them with the warm, soapy water. Use your fingertips to gently roll the bundle back and forth until the fibers start to mesh together. As they do, you can apply more pressure. Continue rolling for about 5 to 10 minutes, until the fibers have tightened up around the pipe cleaner. Rinse the piece with cold water, squeeze the extra water into a towel, and set it on the cooling rack to dry.

3. Cut the piece in half to make two stems.

Felted Snowman

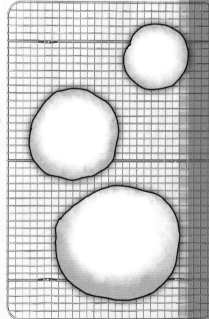

Make this little felted friend to help remind you to always stay cool!

Materials

- 3 white Felted Balls (see step 1)
- 1 orange "carrot" (see step 2)
- Needle
- White and black thread
- Scissors
- 5 black plastic seed beads
- Piece of black Flat Felted Fabric (see page 10)

Steps

1. Follow the steps for the Felted BBs and Balls project on page 15 to make 3 white balls. Make the smallest ball with 20 tufts of roving. For the middle ball, start with 20 tufts, but add about 10 more tufts as you roll. For the largest ball, start with 20 tufts and add about 20 more as you roll. After you rinse the balls and place them on the cooling rack, push down on them so they flatten a bit on the top and bottom.

2. To make a carrot, start with a tuft of orange roving. Follow the steps for rolling a ball on page 15, but roll it into a tiny snake instead of a ball shape.

3. To make the snowman's body, thread the needle with white thread and knot the end. Sew up through the largest ball, then through the middle ball, and finally through the smallest ball. Pull the thread tight and tie a knot at the top. (See sewing tip on page 18.)

4. Cut the carrot nose to the length you need. Sew the cut end to the snowman's face with white thread. Add two bead eyes. Sew three bead buttons down the front of the snowman's body.

5. To make the hat, cut a small rectangle from the fabric. Sew the two shorter edges together with black thread to make a tube. Cut a small circle from the fabric. Make sure it is wider than the tube. Sew this circle onto the top of the snowman's head. Sew the edges of the tube onto the circle.

Wooly Wonders

You may find that you can't predict exactly how a project will come out. Fibers sometimes felt in unexpected ways. You might be surprised when your project ends up looking very different than you pictured it. But that's part of the fun of felting! Try mixing different colors into one ball. Try adding lots of kinds of thread to a felted image. Roll a ball 10 times or 100 times and see the difference. Making art can be like playing. It's a time to use your imagination, take risks, and enjoy the unexpected results.

Try creating some woolly wonders of your own!

What will you make next?

Glossary

absorb (uhb-ZORB) to soak up

alternating (ALL-tur-nay-ting) going back and forth between two things

carding (KAR-ding) the process of untangling and separating wool fibers

compress (kuhm-PRESS) to make something smaller by applying pressure to it

cylindrical (suh-LIN-drih-kuhl) having the shape of a tube

fiber (FY-bur) a tiny strand that makes up a natural material

friction (FRIK-shun) the force created when two surfaces rub together

fulling (FUL-ing) using friction to help fibers shrink and lock together

horizontally (hor-i-ZON-tuh-lee) in a side-to-side direction

nomads (NOH-madz) people who travel from place to place instead of settling in permanent homes

roving (ROH-ving) strands of wool fibers gathered together into long ropes

template (TEM-plit) a pattern used to make the same shape multiple times

vertically (VUR-tuh-klee) in an up-and-down direction

For More Information

Books

Ditchfield, Christin. *The Story Behind Wool*. Chicago: Heinemann Library, 2012.

Kuskowski, Alex. *Cool Needle Felting for Kids: A Fun and Creative Introduction to Fiber Art.* Minneapolis: ABDO Publishing Company, 2015.

Langley, Andrew. *Wool*. New York: Crabtree Publishing Co., 2009.

Macken, JoAnn Early. *Sheep*. Pleasantville, NY: Weekly Reader, 2010.

Nelson, Robin. *From Sheep to Sweater*. Minneapolis: Lerner, 2013.

Web Sites

American Textile History Museum

www.athm.org

Find out more about this museum in Lowell, Massachusetts, which educates visitors on the art and science of textiles through history.

Happy Crafty Family

www.parentingfuneveryday.com/tag/felting-with-children/

Find felting projects and lots of other fun craft ideas at this site.

How Products Are Made: Felt

www.madehow.com/Volume-7/Felt.html

Read more about the history and uses of felt at this informative site.

International Wool Textile Organisation: History of Wool

www.iwto.org/wool/history-of-wool/

Read about the innovations that have made wool such an important part of history.

Index

Bull's-Eye Beads project, 20–22
Bull's-Eye Bracelet project, 23

carding, 6
cooling racks, 9

dowels, 9

Felted BBs and Balls project, 15–16
Felted Flowers project, 24–26
Felted Fruit project, 17–19
Felted Snowman project, 27–28
fiber art, 4–5
Flat Felted Fabric project, 10–13
friction, 8

history, 4–5

Imaginative Image project, 14

Merino wool, 8

netting, 9
nomads, 5

plastic, 9

roving, 6, 8
rubber bands, 9

shears, 6
sheep, 6
soap, 8
supplies, 8–9

tulle, 9

water, 8
workspace, 8

About the Author

Dana Meachen Rau is the author of more than 300 books for children on many topics, including science, history, cooking, and crafts. She creates, experiments, researches, and writes from her home office in Burlington, Connecticut.